# NAMES

## CONTENTS

A Read-about

MEAD · WALLS · O'NEIL · DAWKINS · NEIGHBOUR · RIGDEWAY · DOLITTLE

# NAMES THAT DESCRIBE PEOPLE

ONE of the first things you learn when you are very small is that you have something special that belongs just to you – your name. Have you ever wondered if your name has any meaning?

Long, long ago first names (or given names) were the only names people needed. Villages were small enough for everyone to know each other by name, and there were plenty of names to go around. But gradually, as villages grew and outsiders with the same name moved into town, the need for another name developed.

*The name's BLAINE!*

*GEORGE BASSETT*

Often it was physical appearance that decided this other name. Here are some examples of common last names (or surnames) that once described how people looked: Ball (bald), Cameron (crooked nose), Krauss (curly hair). In all probability the feature that gave this second name to someone applied to other members of the family as well. So it became the family name or surname.

*The chap on the left lives up to his surname Blaine, which means thin. Can you guess what his friend's name means?*

2

The ways in which people behaved also provided some of our last names: Hardy (daring), Hughes (smart), Wilson (determined).

Surnames showing relationship were also an important way of separating two people with the same first name. For example, one child named John would come to be known as John Robertson (John who is Robert's son); the other might be called John Wilson (John who is Will's son). Most names beginning with O' or Mac or ending in son, ing, ich, or kin were formed this way and originally meant "son of".

# SURNAMES FROM PLACES

Many other last names have come from place names. They tell us something about our ancestors' original homeland: Frank (from France), Scott (from Scotland), York (from York, a city in England). Names such as North and Western tell the direction from which a newcomer may have entered the village.

Other surnames tell us where our ancestors lived in their town. Tom, who lived near the pond, may have been known as Tom Atwater (Tom-at-the-water). John, who lived near the middle of the town, became John Middleton.

Lots of other names tell us what the village looked like: Orchard, Marsh, Barn(e)s, Lake, Hill, Stone, Bridges, Wall, Wells.

There may be children in your class whose names have come from places or things in this picture. Other children may find their last names come from similar things in other languages: Lachlan (meaning lake in Scottish) or Lance (which comes from a word relating to land in German).

5

# SURNAMES FROM OCCUPATIONS

Some surnames tell us what our ancestors did for a living. Hunter, Archer, Baker and Miller are easy examples. But some trades are uncommon now, so the surnames that come from them must be explained: Cooper (barrel maker) or Fletcher (arrow maker).

Other names changed spelling over the years, but you can see how some interesting surnames developed: Lederman (leather tanner) or Sherman (sheep shearer).

Names from jobs were handy because a son tended to have the same occupation as his father and grandfather. Today, if your last name is Miller and there is a miller in your family, it is probably just a coincidence.

In fact, you'll find very few surnames to do with modern occupations because people already have their last names. You may know some Drivers, but probably no Pilots. You'll meet Mr Miller and Mrs Weaver but you're unlikely to meet Mrs Engineer or Mr Electrician.

In this village scene you'll see lots of people at work and play. How many activities can you see that may have provided last names?

# GIVEN NAMES

Most parents think long and hard about the name they choose for their baby. It is one of the biggest decisions they will make for their child and will be of lifelong importance.

Most first names are more or less common and have been around for a very long time. Many are from the Bible: James, Jacob, Rebecca and Ruth. Others are names which parents of long ago associated with qualities they wished for their children: David (friend) or Emily (hard worker). Down through the ages, the list has grown as cultures and countries round the world supplied new names.

Still other given names are simply the first or last names of other members of the family or of famous people admired by the baby's parents. Trendy names such as Sky, Willow and Brook reflect some parents' desire to name their children after examples of natural beauty.

Often people acquire names in addition to their given names. Most common are nicknames. These can be shortened forms of the given name: Billy (from William) or Peggy (from Margaret). Names that are affectionately given to people as they grow up are another kind of nickname. Such names as "Apple-cheeks", "Button-nose" and "Half-pint" might well describe a young child, but they have a way of sticking around for years! Do you or any of

LET'S
HIM
AFTER
FATH

YOU COULD CALL HIM JUSTIN. IT'S VERY POPULAR NOW. I ALREADY BABY-SIT A LOT OF OTHERS.

CALL THE BOY 'CASH!' HE MIGHT LIVE UP TO HIS NAME.

HOW ABOUT 'DANIEL' COZ IT SOUNDS NICE WITH DELANY - YOUR LAST NAME.

8

your family or friends have nicknames? It might be interesting to find out how they got them.

If you really don't like your name, you can change it. Many people in show business do this. (Sting's real name is Gordon Sumner and Elton John's real name is Reggie Dwight.) Writers often do this too. They call the name they write under a "nom de plume" or pen name. (Did you know that Dr Seuss' real name is Theodor Geisel?) A name used by a criminal to avoid getting caught is called an "alias". And a famous person might use a false name when travelling "incognito" so that no one will ask for his autograph.

I THINK IT SHOULD BE CALLED 'NOEL' 'COZ IT'S CHRISTMAS!

WHAT ABOUT 'SYDNEY', BECAUSE HE WAS BORN IN SYDNEY.

I WANNA CALL HIM 'SNOOPY' 'COZ I LOVE SNOOPY!

CALL HIM 'PUG' 'COZ HIS NOSE IS SO PUGGY!

**A**   **Abigail** (Hebrew) my father rejoices

**Alice** (Germanic) kind, noble

**Alison** — a form of Alice: kind, noble

**Amanda** (Latin) lovable

**Amy** (Old French) to love

**Andrea** (Greek) brave

**Angela** (Greek) angel

**Ann** (Hebrew) grace, God has been gracious

**Annabel** (Scottish) lovable, beautiful Anna

**B**   **Barbara** (Greek) stranger, foreigner

**Beth** — from Elizabeth: God is satisfied

**Bianca** — Italian form of Blanche: (French) fair, white

**Bonnie** (Scottish) good, pretty

**Brenda** (Norse) sword

**Bridget** (Celtic) strength, the high one

**C**   **Candy** — from Candace: (Greek/Latin) white, glowing

**Caroline** (Old French) song of joy

**Casey** (Irish) brave

**Cassandra** (Greek) helper of mankind

**Catherine** (Greek) pure

**Cherie** (French) dear

**Christine** (Old English) she is christened

**Cindy** (Greek) moon goddess

**Claire** (Latin) clear, bright

**Crystal** (Greek) frost, clear ice

**D**   **Dalila** (African) gentle

**Danielle** (French) God is my judge

**Deborah** (Hebrew) bee

**Deirdre** (Gaelic) sorrow

**Diana** (Latin) moon goddess

**Donna** (Spanish/Italian) lady

**E**   **Eleanor** — French form of Helen: (Greek) light, bright one

**Elizabeth** (Hebrew) God is satisfied

**Emily** (Latin) hard worker, easy to get along with

**Emma** (Old German) whole, universal

**Erica** (Germanic) heather, rule

**Erin** (Celtic) Ireland, peace

**F**   **Farrah** (Old English) pleasant, beautiful

**Felicity** (Latin) happy

**Fleur** (French) flower

**G**   **Gail** (Old English) merry, lively

**Gemma** (Italian) gem

**Gina** — from Angela: angel

**Greer** (Greek) watchful

**H** **Hannah** (Hebrew) grace, God has been gracious

**Hayley** (Old English) high meadow

**Heidi** — from Adelaide: (Old German) noble, kind

**Holly** (Old English) holly

**I** **Ingrid** (Old Norse) daughter

**Isabel** — French form of Elizabeth: God is satisfied

**J** **Jacqueline** (Hebrew) may God protect, supplanter

**Jade** (Spanish) jade stone

**Jaime** (Spanish) love

**Jane** (Hebrew) gracious gift of God

**Jasmine** (Persian) jasmine

**Jennifer** (Celtic) white wave

**Jessica** (Hebrew) gracious gift of God

**Jillian** (Greek/Latin) youthful

**Joanna** (Hebrew) gracious gift of God

**Jocelyn** (Latin) merry

**Jodie** — from Judith: (Hebrew) praised

**Joy** (Middle English) joy

**Juanita** — Spanish form of Jane: gracious gift of God

**Julia** (Latin) youthful, soft hair

**K** **Kamala** (Indian) lotus

**Kate** — from Katherine: pure

**Katherine** (Greek) pure

**Kathleen** — Irish form of Katherine: pure

**Keely** (Celtic) beautiful

**Keiko** (Japanese) pretty

**Kelly** (Irish) from the surname Kelly

**Kerry** (Celtic) dark

**Kimberley** (Old English) from a royal or famous place

**Kiri** (Polynesian) bark of a tree

**Kirsty** — Scottish form of Christine: she is christened

**Kylie** (Aboriginal) boomerang

**L** **Laura** (Latin) laurel, victory

**Lauren** — from Laura: laurel, victory

**Lee** (Old English) meadow

**Leilani** (Hawaiian) heavenly flower

**Libby** — from Elizabeth: God is satisfied

**Lisa** — from Elizabeth: God is satisfied

**Liza** — from Elizabeth: God is satisfied

**Lori** (Latin) victory

11

# Even more

Lucy (Latin) light

**M** Madeleine (Aramaic) tower

Mandy — from Amanda: lovable

Margaret (Greek) pearl

Maria — Latin form of Mary: wanted child

Mary (Hebrew) wanted child

Matilda (Old German) strength, battle

Megan — Welsh form of Margaret: pearl

Melanie (Greek) black

Melissa (Greek) honeybee, sweet

Meryl — from Merle: (Latin) blackbird

Mia (Italian) mine

Michelle (Hebrew) who is like God

Mimi — French nickname

Molly — Irish form of Mary: wanted child

**N** Nancy (Hebrew) grace

Nani (Polynesian) beautiful

Naomi (Hebrew) pleasant

Natalie (Latin) Christmas Day

Nicole (Greek) victory, the people

**P** Page (Old English) a page of the court

Pamela (Greek) honey

Paula (Latin) small

Peggy — from Margaret: pearl

Polly — from Molly and Mary: wanted child

**R** Rachel (Hebrew) ewe

Rebecca (Hebrew) cow

Robyn (Teutonic) fame, bright

Rochelle (French) rock, restful

**S** Sabrina (Latin) legendary English princess

Sachiko (Japanese) joy

Sally — from Sarah: princess

Samantha (Aramaic) good listener

Sandra (Greek) helper of man

Sarah (Hebrew) princess

Shona — Irish form of Jane: gracious gift of God

Stacey — from Anastasia: (Greek) arise again

Stephanie (Greek) crown

Susan (Hebrew) lily

**T** Tabitha (Aramaic) gazelle

Tammy — from Tamara: (Slavonic/Hebrew) palm tree

Tara (Gaelic) hill

Tina — from Christine: she is christened

Toni — from Antonia: (Latin) flourishing, too many to measure

Tracey — from Teresa: (Greek) harvester

Tricia — from Patricia: (Latin) well born, noble

**V** Vanessa (Latin) butterfly, full of grace

**W** Wendy (Welsh) brows of white

**Z** Zara — Arabic form of Sarah: princess

Zoe (Greek) life

**A** **Aaron** (Hebrew) high mountain, the exalted one

**Adam** (Hebrew) man of red earth

**Alan** (Celtic) harmony, noble, handsome

**Alastair** — Scottish form of Alexander: helper of men

**Alexander** (Greek) helper of man

**Andrew** (Celtic) one choice

**Angus** (Celtic) one choice

**Anthony** (Latin) strong, flourishing

**Ari** (Hebrew) lion

**B** **Barry** (Celtic) spear, bear

**Benjamin** (Hebrew) son of the right hand, son of the south

**Brad** (Old English) broad meadow

**Brendan** (Old Irish) sword

**Brian** (Celtic) hill, strong

**Bruce** (Old French) from Brieuse in Normandy

**Bryce** (Celtic) St Brice, a French bishop

**C** **Callum** (Scots Gaelic) follower of St Columb

**Cameron** (Scots Gaelic) crooked nose

**Carlos** (Spanish) man

**Casey** (Irish) brave, courageous

**Chad** (Celtic) war

**Chaim** (Hebrew) life

**Charles** (Old German) man, supporter

**Christian** (Latin) a follower of Christ

**Christopher** (Greek) bearer of Christ

**Colin** (Scottish Gaelic) young dog, youth

**Cory** (Greek) shortened form of Corydon: lark

**Craig** (Gaelic) mountain crag

**D** **Damian** (Greek) to tame

**Daniel** (Hebrew) judged by God

**Darren** (Greek) follower of Dorus: a classical architect

**Daryl** (French) loved

**David** (Hebrew) darling

**Denis** (Greek) of Dionysos, Greek god of wine

**Derek** (Old German) ruler of the people

**Donald** (Celtic) mighty

**Dougal** (Celtic) dark stranger

**Duncan** (Old Irish) brown warrior

**Dustin** (Old German) valiant, brave

**Dylan** (Celtic) son of the wave

**E** **Edward** (Old English) rich, happy

**Eric** (Teutonic/Old Norse) kingly

**F** **Fraser** (Old French) ash tree

**Fred** — from Frederick: (Old German) peace, ruler

**G** **Gary** (Celtic) hunting dog

**Gavin** (Welsh) hawk

**George** (Greek) farmer

**Glen** (Gaelic) valley

**Graham** (Old English) gray and gravelly homestead

**Grant** (Latin/Old French) large, tall

**Greg** — from Gregory: (Greek) watchful

**H** **Hal** — from Harold: (Old Norse) army power

**Hamish** — Gaelic form of James: may God protect, supplanter

**Haydon** (Old English) heather hill

**Hemi** — Maori form of James: may God protect, supplanter

**Hugh** (Germanic) heart, mind

**I** **Ian** — Scottish form of John: gracious gift of God

**Isaac** (Hebrew) God may smile upon me, laughter

**J** **Jack** — from John: gracious gift of God

**Jacob** (Hebrew) may God protect, supplanter

**James** (Hebrew) may God protect, supplanter

**Jason** (Hebrew) healer

**Jay** (American) jay bird

**Jed** — from Jedidiah: (Hebrew) friend of God

**Jeff** — from Geoffrey: (Germanic) God, peace, district of land

**Jeremy** — from Jeremiah: (Hebrew) may God raise up

**Jesse** (Hebrew) God exists

**Joel** (Hebrew) Jehovah is God

**John** (Hebrew) gracious gift of God

**Jonathan** (Hebrew) God has given us a son

**José** — Spanish form of Joseph: (Hebrew) God has added a child

**Joshua** (Hebrew) God is my help

**Juan** — Spanish form of John: gracious gift of God

**Justin** (Latin) just, upright

**K** **Kane** (Welsh) beautiful

**Keith** (Scottish Gaelic) wind, woods

**Kenneth** (Gaelic) handsome

**Kerry** (Gaelic) dark

**Kevin** (Celtic) handsome at birth

**Kirby** (Germanic) village with a church

**Kirk** (Old Norse) church

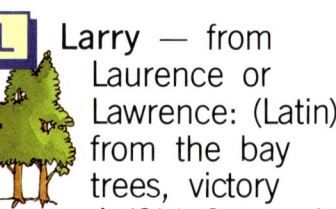

**Kit** — from Christopher: bearer of Christ

**Kyle** (Gaelic) from a district in Scotland

**L** **Larry** — from Laurence or Lawrence: (Latin) from the bay trees, victory

**Leonard** (Old German) lion, hardy, bold

**Leroy** (Old French) the king

**Liam** — Irish form of William: will, helmet

**Lloyd** (Welsh) gray, brown

**Luke** (Latin) light

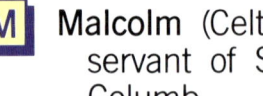

**M** **Malcolm** (Celtic) servant of St Columb

**Marco** — Italian form of Mark: of Mars, God of War

**Mark** (Latin) of Mars, God of War

**Martin** (Latin) of Mars

**Matthew** (Hebrew) gift of God

**Max** (Latin) the greatest

**Michael** (Hebrew) who is like God

**Murray** (Old English) merry, seaboard settlement

**Nathaniel** (Hebrew) gift of God

**Neil** (Irish) champion

**Nicholas** (Greek) victory, the people

**Nigel** (Latin/Irish) dark, champion

**Noel** (Latin/Old French) Christmas

**Oliver** (Latin) olive tree

**Pablo** — Spanish form of Paul: small

**Patrick** (Latin) nobleman

**Paul** (Latin) small

**Pedro** — Spanish form of Peter: rock

**Peter** (Greek) rock

**Philip** (Greek) lover of horses

**Quentin** (Latin) the fifth

**Randall** (Old English) shield, wolf

**Rex** (Latin) king

**Richard** (Teutonic) ruler

**Robert** (Teutonic) fame, bright

**Roger** (Teutonic) fame, spear

**Ross** (Scottish Gaelic/Old German) peninsula, fame

**Roy** (Celtic/Old French) red, king

**Ryan** (Latin/Celtic) laughing, little king

**Samuel** (Hebrew) name of God

**Scott** (Celtic) from Scotland

**Sean** — Irish form of John: gracious gift of God

**Shane** — Irish form of John: gracious gift of God

**Shannon** (Irish) old river

**Simon** (Hebrew) God has heard, listening

**Skip** (Old Norse) ship master

**Stanley** (Old English) stony clearing, field

**Stephen** (Greek) crown

**Stuart** (Old English) in charge of the house

**Ted** — from Edward: rich, happy ·

**Thomas** (Aramaic) twin

**Timothy** (Greek) respecting God

**Trevor** (Welsh) big village

**Troy** (Irish) son of a foot soldier

**Wade** (Old English) one who goes wading

**Walter** (Old German) rule, folk, army

**Warren** (Old English) protector

**Wayne** (Old English) wagonner

**William** (Old German) will, helmet

**Wiremu** — Maori form of William: will, helmet

**Zachary** (Hebrew) God has remembered

**Zane** — a form of John: gracious gift of God

THROUGH the ages, various cultures have built up traditions for naming a child. In most countries the law says that parents must register a child's birth and name. The actual giving of a name may be done by simply filling in a

**TOP LEFT**
During a confirmation service, this girl receives a special saint's name of her choosing.

**BOTTOM LEFT**
A wedding ceremony in Fiji. In most countries it is the tradition for the new bride to use her husband's last name as her new surname. Many brides now prefer to keep their family name or to combine it with that of their husband.

form at a Registry of Births, or there may be a church baptism followed by a family celebration. Further Christian names may be given at ceremonies such as confirmation and ordination.

**BELOW LEFT**
At a Registry of Births, a mother and father fill in a form soon after their baby's birth. This form will record such details as the child's full name, birthdate and place of birth.

**BELOW**
A priest announces a young baby's given name during a church baptism.

BROWNLEE

# Family

**Y**OU may not have thought of this, but your name and your family history may entitle you to use a family "symbol". Coats of arms and tartans are well known examples of family identification that developed long ago in Europe and have survived through the ages. From tattoos to totem poles, people round the world had their own ways of showing family groups. Special designs on shields and masks, clothing, jewelry and blankets mean something important to the people who created them.

Crests and mottos on ancient coats of arms remind us of good qualities (such as leadership or courage) or deeds (such as conqueror or landowner) of a famous early member of the family. These family symbols came to be used with pride by later members of the family to inspire them to try to do the same worthy deeds as their ancestor.

In much the same way, kilts, scarves, tam-o'-shanters, etc. in plaid designs have for hundreds of years shown membership of Scottish clans or families. Campbell, Stewart, MacGregor and other tartans are worn with pride and pleasure by official members of these Scottish clans as well as by other people.

All these symbols are ways of saying, "We belong to a clan, a tribe, a family." However, the use of these symbols is not as common now as in

# Crests

years gone by. Today, it's mostly ties and tieclips, rings, pennants, scarves, badges and T-shirts that tell the world, "I'm part of the gang — and proud of it!"

## LET'S MAKE A FAMILY SHIELD

If you don't have a family coat of arms, you could use some of the symbols on this page to make one. Think up a motto such as "Truth and Courage" or just put your surname on your shield. Make it bright and colourful and display it proudly.

BRAVE    SPEED    STRONG    HUMOUR    TALL    PATIENT    GOOD SPORT

ARTISTIC    KNITTER    QUIET    CHEERFUL    WISE    BEAUTIFUL    BUSY

19

# FOR THE RECORD

## THE OLDEST NAME

The oldest name in the world is said to have belonged to an ancient Egyptian king. His name was recorded by the hieroglyphic symbol for a scorpion.

## THE LONGEST NAME

The longest name to appear on a birth certificate belongs to a little girl in Texas named Rhoshandiatellyneshiaunneveshenk Williams. Her father later filed a longer version of her name, making her first name 1,019 letters long!

## THE MOST GIVEN NAMES

The most given names belong to Tracey Nelson in England, who was christened with 140 of her parents' favourite names.

## MOST COMMON NAMES

The most common family name in the world is Chang, used by about 10% of all the people of China. That's about 73,000,000 people — and that's a lot of Changs! You've probably already guessed that the most common surname in the English language is plain old Smith. Christopher and Sarah are the most popular first names. How many Christophers and Sarahs do you know?

## NAMES FROM PLACES

We learned earlier in this book that long ago many people took their surnames from the land around them. But so far we don't know of anyone named Taumatawhakatangihanga koauauotamatea (turipukakapi — maungahoronuku) pokaiwhenua-kitanatahu, a mouthful from New Zealand which means in the Maori language, "the hill whereon was played the flute of Tamatea, circumnavigator of lands, for his lady love".

# FUN WITH NAMES

While we know that many generations ago people sometimes took their surnames from their trade, it's mostly just a coincidence if this occurs today. Do you know anyone whose name fits the job?

| MRS WRENCH The Dentist | | P.O. BOX The Postman | | Mr BASHAM The Builder | | I.M. FITT The Jogger | |
|---|---|---|---|---|---|---|---|

The name of the game match-up: who does what?

Some names take on a new meaning altogether when a person marries. Believe it or not, Mary Woolley married John Lamb and became Mary Woolley Lamb. A bride named Rose might marry a man whose surname is Budd or Thorn and become Rose Budd or Rose Thorn.

# CRAZY BOOKS

# NAMESEARCH

How many first and last names can you find? You may spot them running backwards or forwards, up and down, sidewise or diagonally. Here are some of the names to look for: Ann, Steve, Donna, West, Krauss, Ellen and Fletcher. (Hint: There are at least 24 more!)

```
H S I M O N R W E R D
T A C N M W E A V E R
A N N O D H L L N H O
K D T J T D L L U C Y
Y R R T I T I A N T S
L A A R G E M N D E T
I M G U A N N E L L E
E N M A S R I C H F V
I F F E T S E W E V E
```

# CONCLUSION

You've seen in this book that names can be a serious business and sometimes a bit of fun too. Now you know that most names have a meaning and a history all their own. You will enjoy telling your friends and family the "story" of their names. And when you want to find out more information about this fascinating subject, there will be lots of books about names waiting for you in your local library.